To: _____

From: _____

Date: _____

Published in the United States by Random House Children's Books,
a division of Penguin Random House LLC, New York.
The artwork that appears herein was adapted from the book *Are You My Mother?*,
copyright © 1960 by P. D. Eastman, and copyright renewed 1988 by Mary L. Eastman.

Random House and the colophon are registered trademarks of Penguin Random House LLC.

Visit us on the Web!
rhcbooks.com

Educators and librarians, for a variety of teaching tools, visit us at
RHTeachersLibrarians.com

ISBN 978-0-593-12118-4

MANUFACTURED IN CHINA   10 9 8 7 6 5 4 3 2 1   First Edition

You Are My Mother

INSPIRED BY
P. D. Eastman's
Are You My Mother?

Random House New York

You are
my mother.

You loved me and took care of me even before I was born.

You were **always**
there for me . . .

... even when
we were apart.

You gave me
the **best start**
in life!

When
I took
my **first**
step . . .

. . . you were
not far away.

You gave me
the **confidence**
to meet new
people . . .

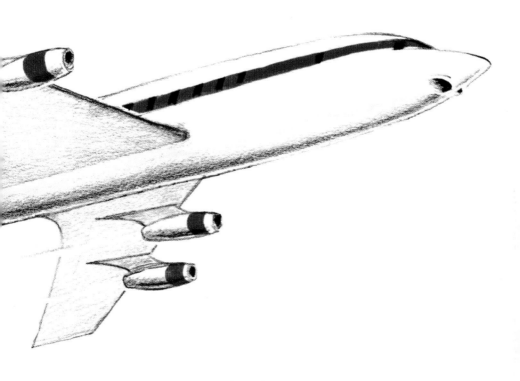

. . . visit new places . . .

. . . and try
new things!

There is no one
who makes me
happier.

There is no one
I care for more.
**You are
my mother,
and I love you.**